Manchester United Quiz Book

101 Questions To Test Your Knowledge Of This World Famous Club

Published by Glowworm Press
7 Nuffield Way
Abingdon OX14 1RL

By Chris Carpenter

Manchester United Football Club

This book contains one hundred and one informative and entertaining trivia questions with multiple choice answers. With 101 questions, some easy, some harder, this book will test your knowledge and memory of the club's long and successful history.

You will be asked a wide range of original questions on a wide range of topics associated with Manchester United Football Club for you to test yourself. You will be quizzed on players, legends, managers, opponents, transfer deals, trophies, records, honours, fixtures, terrace songs and much more, guaranteeing you a fun experience. This educational Manchester United Quiz Book will provide the ultimate in entertainment for all loyal Manchester United supporters.

2019-20 Season Edition

FOREWORD

When I was asked to write a foreword to this book I was extremely flattered.

I have known the author Chris Carpenter for many years and his knowledge of facts and figures is phenomenal.

His love for football and his flair for writing quiz books makes him the ideal man to pay tribute to my great love Manchester United Football Club.

This book came about as a result of a challenge in a Lebanese restaurant of all places!

I do hope you enjoy the book.

Michael Robertson

Let's start with some relatively easy questions.

1. When were the club founded?
   A. 1874
   B. 1876
   C. 1878

2. What is Manchester United's nickname?
   A. Boys in Red
   B. Little Devils
   C. The Red Devils

3. Who has made the most appearances for the club in total?
   A. Bobby Charlton
   B. Ryan Giggs
   C. Paul Scholes

4. Who has made the most *League* appearances for the club?
   A. Ryan Giggs
   B. Billy Meredith
   C. Edwin van der Sar

5. Who is the club's record goal scorer?
   A. Bobby Charlton
   B. Denis Law
   C. Wayne Rooney

OK, so here are the answers to the first five questions. If you get all five right, you are doing very well so far, but don't get too cocky, as the questions get harder.

A1. The club was founded as Newton Heath LYR football club in 1878, and turned professional in 1885, before joining the Football League in 1892. After a brush with bankruptcy in 1901, the club reformed as Manchester United in 1902.

A2. Manchester United's official nickname is The Red Devils.

A3. The record appearance maker is Ryan Giggs, who made an incredible 963 appearances for the club. He had 150 different team mates!

A4. Ryan Giggs has made the most League appearances for a player, with 611.

A5. The club's record goal scorer is Wayne Rooney who scored 253 goals in 559 games between 2004 and 2017.

6. Who has scored the most penalties for the club?
   A. David Beckham
   B. Eric Cantona
   C. Ruud van Nistelrooy

7. Who is the fastest ever goal scorer for the club?
   A. Andy Cole
   B. Ryan Giggs
   C. Wayne Rooney

8. Who or what is the club mascot?
   A. Dennis the Devil
   B. Fred the Red
   C. Lucifer

9. What is the highest number of goals that Manchester United has scored in a league season?
   A. 97
   B. 99
   C. 103

10. What is the fewest number of goals that Manchester United has conceded in a league season?
    A. 22
    B. 24
    C. 26

A6. The player who has scored the most penalties for the club is Ruud van Nistelrooy who scored 18 out of 22 - 82% successful spot kicks.

A7. Manchester United's fastest goal ever was scored by Ryan Giggs against Southampton in the Premier League at Old Trafford on 18th November 1995. Giggsy scored just after 15 seconds of play.

A8. The club mascot is Fred the Red. He is a popular figure that goofs around before home matches and he wears a shirt with the number 55 on the back.

A9. The most league goals scored by the club in a season was 103 in both the 1956–57 and 1958–59 seasons.

A10. The fewest number of goals conceded in a season was 22 in the 2007–08 season

OK, let's have some ground related questions.

11. Where does Manchester United play their home games?
    A. City of Manchester Stadium
    B. Maine Road
    C. Old Trafford

12. What is the stadium's capacity?
    A. 74,994
    B. 75,994
    C. 76,994

13. What is the home end of the ground known as?
    A. The East Stand
    B. The Stretford End
    C. The United Road Stand

14. What is the club's record attendance?
    A. 74,980
    B. 75,809
    C. 76,098

15. What is the name of the road the ground is on?
    A. Kings Road
    B. Urban Road
    C. Warwick Road

Here are your answers to the stadium related questions.

A11. In February 1909, Old Trafford was named as the home of Manchester United.

A12. According to the stadium specific page on Wikipedia, the current stadium capacity of Old Trafford is 74,994. It is the second largest football stadium in the United Kingdom after Wembley Stadium.

A13. The best-known stand at Old Trafford is the West Stand, also known as the Stretford End. Traditionally, the stand is where the hard-core United fans are located, and also the ones who make the most noise.

A14. The record home attendance at Old Trafford for a match involving Manchester United is 76,098 for a Premier League game against Blackburn Rovers on 31st March 2007. The record attendance at Old Trafford ever is 76,962 for an FA Cup semi-final played between Wolverhampton Wanderers and Grimsby Town on 25th March 1939.

A15. Old Trafford is located just off the north end of the Warwick Road in Trafford.

16. Which stand has the biggest capacity?
    A. The East Stand
    B. The Sir Alex Ferguson Stand
    C. The Stretford End

17. What is the size of the pitch?
    A. 111 yards × 75 yards
    B. 113 yards × 76 yards
    C. 115 yards x 74 yards

18. What is the nickname of Old Trafford, as coined by Bobby Charlton?
    A. Theatre of Despair
    B. Theatre of Doom
    C. Theatre of Dreams

19. Which of these is a well-known pub near the ground?
    A. Bishop Beckett
    B. Bishop Blaize
    C. Bishop Vesey

20. What is Manchester United's training ground better known as?
    A. Barrington
    B. Carrington
    C. Harrington

A16. The Sir Alex Ferguson Stand, formerly known as the United Road stand and the North Stand, can hold about 26,000 spectators, all seated; the most of the four stands.

A17. The pitch at the ground measures approximately 115 yards long by 74 yards wide. In metric it is 105 metres long by 68 metres wide, with a few metres/yards of run-off space on each side.

A18. Old Trafford was nicknamed the Theatre of Dreams by Bobby Charlton in 1978, although it wasn't really picked up by the media until the mid-1990s.

A19. There are two main areas for pubs immediately around Old Trafford with The Trafford and the Bishop Blaize probably being the two closest boozers to the ground. Both pubs are always packed with supporters, so be prepared to queue for a pint.

A20. The Aon Training Complex (formerly the Trafford Training Centre) is usually referred to as Carrington is the club's training facility and academy headquarters.

Now we move onto another set of questions.

21. What is the club's record win in any
    competition?
    A. 9-0
    B. 9-1
    C. 10-0

22. Who did they beat?
    A. Aberdeen
    B. Anderlecht
    C. Atletico Madrid

23. In which season?
    A. 1956-57
    B. 1957-58
    C. 1958-59

24. What is the club's record win in the League?
    A. 9-0
    B. 9-1
    C. 9-2

25. Who did they beat?
    A. Ipswich Town
    B. Swindon Town
    C. Yeovil Town

Here is the latest set of answers.

A21. The club's record win is 10-0.

A22. Manchester United beat Anderlecht 10-0 in the European Cup Preliminary Round, second leg, 26th September 1956.

A23. The match took place on 26th September 1956, so it was the 1956/57 season.

A24. Manchester United's record League win is 9-0.

A25. Manchester United defeated Ipswich Town 9-0 in their record League win.

26. When was the club's record league win?
  A. 1995-96
  B. 1996-97
  C. 1997-98

27. What is the club's record defeat?
  A. 1-7
  B. 0-7
  C. 0-8

28. Who was the record defeat against?
  A. Aston Villa
  B. Blackburn Rovers
  C. Wolverhampton Wanderers

29. Who scored the winning goal in the 1999 Champions League Final?
  A. Jesper Blomqvist
  B. Ole Gunnar Solskjaer
  C. Teddy Sheringham

30. Who has scored the most hat tricks for Manchester United?
  A. Denis Law
  B. Sammy McIlroy
  C. Ruud van Nistelrooy

A26. Manchester United trounced Ipswich Town 9-0 on 4th March 1995 during the 1995/96 season.

A27. Manchester United's record defeat is 0-7.

A28. Aston Villa, Blackburn Rovers and Wolverhampton Wanderers have somehow all beaten Manchester United 7-0. Give yourself a bonus point if you knew that. Blackburn Rovers won in April 1926; Aston Villa in December 1930 and Wolverhampton Wanderers in December 1931.

A29. Ole Gunnar Solskjaer scored the important winner in the 93rd minute of the 1999 Champions League Final to help Manchester United beat Bayern Munich 2-1 and win the trophy.

A30. Denis Law scored an incredible 18 hat tricks for the club, and he was only with the club from 3rd November 1962 to 17th April 1971.

Now some questions about the club's trophies.

31. How many times has Manchester United won the Premier League?
    A. 11
    B. 12
    C. 13

32. How many times has Manchester United won the League title in total - Premier League and First Division?
    A. 18
    B. 19
    C. 20

33. When did the club win their first League title?
    A. 1908
    B. 1918
    C. 1928

34. How many times has Manchester United won the FA Cup?
    A. 11
    B. 12
    C. 13

35. How many times have they won the League Cup?
    A. 3
    B. 4
    C. 5

Here is the latest set of answers.

A31. Manchester United has won the Premier League a record 13 times since its inception. 1992–93, 1993–94, 1995–96, 1996–97, 1998–99, 1999–2000, 2000–01, 2002–03, 2006–07, 2007–08, 2008–09, 2010–11 and 2012–13.

A32. Manchester United has won a record twenty English titles, so that's thirteen Premier League Titles and seven Division One Titles.

A33. The club won its first League title in 1908.

A34. Manchester United has won the FA Cup twelve times: - 1909, 1948, 1963, 1977, 1983, 1985, 1990, 1994, 1996, 1999, 2004 and 2016.

A35. Manchester United has won the League Cup five times: - 1992, 2006, 2009, 2010 and 2017.

36. How many times has the club won the European Cup / Champions League?
    A. 2
    B. 3
    C. 4

37. Who was the last captain to lift the League trophy?
    A. Ryan Giggs
    B. Gary Neville
    C. Nemanja Vidić

38. Who was the last captain to lift the FA Cup?
    A. Roy Keane
    B. Ruud van Nistelrooy
    C. Charlie Roberts

39. Who was the last captain to lift the League Cup?
    A. Patrice Evra
    B. Paul Schole
    C. Chris Smalling

40. Who was the last captain to lift the Champions League?
    A. Patrice Evra
    B. Rio Ferdinand
    C. Owen Hargreaves

A36. Man United have won the European Cup / Champions League three times: - 1968, 1999 and 2008.

A37. The last captain to lift the League trophy was Nemanja Vidić. Manchester United won their 13th Premier League title and 20th English title overall by defeating Aston Villa 3–0 at Old Trafford at the end of the 2012-2013 season.

A38. The last captain to lift the FA Cup was Wayne Rooney after Manchester United beat Crystal Palace 2-1 after extra time at Wembley Stadium on 21st May 2016.

A39. The last captain to lift the League Cup was Chris Smalling after Manchester United beat Southampton 3-2 at Wembley on 26th February 2017.

A40. The last captain to lift the Champions League trophy was Rio Ferdinand after Manchester United beat Chelsea 6-5 on penalties, after the game finished 1-1 after 90 minutes, in Moscow on 21st May 2008.

I hope you're having fun, and getting most of the answers right.

41. What is the record transfer fee paid?
    A. £81.3 million
    B. £85.3 million
    C. £89.3 million

42. Who was the record transfer fee paid for?
    A. Harry Maguire
    B. Angel Di Maria
    C. Paul Pogba

43. What is the record transfer fee received?
    A. £60 million
    B. £70 million
    C. £80 million

44. Who was the record transfer fee received for?
    A. Romelu Lukaku
    B. Ruud van Nistelrooy
    C. Cristiano Ronaldo

45. Who has won the most international caps whilst a Manchester United player?
    A. Bobby Charlton
    B. Wayne Rooney
    C. Edwin van der Sar

Here are the answers to the last set of questions.

A41. Manchester United's record signing fee is £89.3 million (€105 million) in August 2016.

A42. Manchester United's record signing is Paul Pogba who re-signed for the club from Juventus for a British record fee of £89.3 million. This superseded the previous record of £59.7 million paid to Real Madrid for Ángel Di María in August 2014.

A43. In July 2009 Manchester United received £80 million for a superstar.

A44. The club's record sale was of course Cristiano Ronaldo who went to Real Madrid.

A45. Sir Bobby Charlton holds the record for most international caps whilst a United player, winning 106 caps at the club. Wayne Rooney won a total of 119 caps for England, 17 whilst paying for Everton and 102 whilst playing for Manchester United.

46. Who has scored the most international goals whilst a Manchester United player?
    A. Bobby Charlton
    B. Ryan Giggs
    C. Wayne Rooney

47. Who is the youngest player ever to represent the club?
    A. Steve Coppell
    B. David Gaskell
    C. Chris Smalling

48. Who is the youngest ever goalscorer?
    A. Nicky Butt
    B. Rafael
    C. Norman Whiteside

49. Who is the oldest player ever to represent the club?
    A. Ryan Giggs
    B. Billy Meredith
    C. Edwin van der Sar

50. Who is Manchester United's oldest ever goal scorer?
    A. Ryan Giggs
    B. Mark Hughes
    C. Teddy Sheringham

A46. Bobby Charlton scored 49 goals (all goals scored whilst at Manchester United) and Wayne Rooney scored 53 goals (9 whilst at Everton and 44 times whilst at Manchester United) in total for England.

A47. The youngest player ever to represent the club was David Gaskell who made his debut against Manchester City in a Charity Shield match aged just 16 years 19 days on 24th October 1956.

A48. The youngest player to score for Manchester United is Norman Whiteside. Whiteside began his career at Manchester United, signing professional forms in 1982 at the age of 17 and quickly became a key member of the side. He scored 68 goals in 278 league appearances for the club.

A49. Billy Meredith is the oldest player ever to represent the club; he was aged 46 years and 281 days when he appeared against Derby County on 7th May 1921.

A50. Ryan Giggs is the oldest player ever to score for the club. He was aged 39 years and 86 days when he scored in a 2-0 victory over Queens Park Rangers on 23rd February 2013.

Here we go with the next set of questions.

51. Who was the first Manchester United player to play for England?
    A. Bobby Charlton
    B. Alf Schofield
    C. Harry Stafford

52. Who is the club's longest serving manager of all time?
    A. Sir Alex Ferguson
    B. Ernest Magnall
    C. Jack Robson

53. Who is the so called choirmaster at Old Trafford?
    A. Pete Boyle
    B. Pete Coyle
    C. Pete Doyle

54. What is the match day programme?
    A. Devils news
    B. Man United FC - The Official Match Day Programme
    C. United Review

55. What is the club's official twitter account?
    A. @ManU
    B. @ManUnited
    C. @ManUtd

Here is the latest set of answers.

A51. The first Manchester United player to play for England was Bobby Charlton who made his debut in 1958, and made a total of 106 appearances with 49 goals. He famously helped England to win the 1966 World Cup.

A52. The longest serving manager at the club is of course Sir Alex Ferguson – 26 years, 194 days. He was appointed on 6th November 1986 and resigned in May 2013.

A53. Pete Boyle is an MUTV correspondent, fanzine contributor and choirmaster who has been responsible for writing many songs sung by the fans over the years. Amongst his many compositions are "We'll drink a drink a drink to Eric The King" to the tune of Lily the Pink, and the incomparable "Neville, Neville, your future's immense" to the tune of Rebel Rebel.

A54. The catchy name of the Manchester United match day programme is United Review - The Official Match day Programme of Manchester United Football Club.

A55. @ManUtd is the club's official twitter account. It has over 20 million followers and it tweets multiple times daily.

56. Which of these is a Manchester United fanzine?
    A. Glory Glory
    B. MUFC
    C. United We Stand

57. What symbol is on the club crest?
    A. A bandana
    B. A devil
    C. A football

58. Who started the 2019-20 season as manager?
    A. Louis van Gaal
    B. Jose Mourinho
    C. Ole Gunnar Solskjaer

59. Who is considered as Manchester United's main rivals?
    A. Arsenal
    B. Chelsea
    C. Liverpool

60. What could be regarded as the club's most well-known song?
    A. Glory Glory Man United
    B. United are the team for me
    C. United Calypso

A56. United we stand is probably the best known of the Manchester United fanzines. It first appeared on the streets of Manchester in the autumn of 1989. United We Stand often works with two other well-known Manchester United fanzines: - Red Issue and Red News.

A57. The Manchester United badge has featured a devil symbol since 1970.

A58. Ole Gunnar Solskjaer started the 2019-20 season as manager.

A59. The Liverpool – Manchester United rivalry is a footballing rivalry which can be considered to be one of the biggest rivalries between clubs anywhere in the world.

A60. Manchester United fans have sung many great songs over the years, and have been singing Glory Glory Man United regularly since the early 1960s.

I hope you're learning some new facts about the Red Devils. Let's give you some easy questions.

61. What is the traditional colour of the home shirt?
    A. Red
    B. White
    C. Blue

62. What is the traditional colour of the away shirt?
    A. Blue
    B. Green
    C. White

63. Who is the current club sponsor?
    A. AIG
    B. AON
    C. General Motors

64. Who was the first club sponsor?
    A. AIG
    B. Sharp Electronics
    C. Vodafone

65. Who supplies kit to the first team?
    A. Adidas
    B. Nike
    C. Umbro

Here is the latest set of answers.

A61. The traditional colour of the home shirt is of course red. If you got that wrong, what are you doing reading this book!

A62. The traditional colour of the away shirt is white.

A63. In July 2012, United signed a seven year deal with the American automotive corporation General Motors, which replaced Aon as the shirt sponsor from the 2014-15 season onwards. The $80 million a year shirt deal features the logo of General Motors brand Chevrolet.

A64. In an initial five-year deal worth £500,000, Sharp Electronics became the club's first shirt sponsor at the beginning of the 1982-83 season.

A65. Manchester United's kit is currently supplied by Adidas.

66. Who is currently the club chairman?
    A. Richard Arnold
    B. Avram Glazer and Joel Glazer
    C. Ed Woodward

67. Who was the club's first foreign signing?
    A. Nikola Jovanović
    B. William Prunier
    C. Carlos Sartori

68. Who was the club's first black player?
    A. Vivian Anderson
    B. Remi Moses
    C. Tony Whelan

69. Who was the club's first match in the league against?
    A. Blackburn Rovers
    B. Bolton Wanderers
    C. Burnley

70. Where did the club finish in the Premier League at the end of the 2018-19 season?
    A. 4th
    B. 5th
    C. 6th

A66. The club's co-chairmen are Avram Glazer and Joel Glazer. Edward Woodward is the Chief Executive.

A67. Italian born Carlos Sartori was the first foreign player in the history of Manchester United, coming on as a substitute away at Tottenham Hotspur on 9th October 1968.

A68. Tony Whelan played for United in a series of friendlies in 1970, but he never played a competitive match for the club. Remi Moses was however the first black player to make a competitive appearance for the club, making his debut on 12th September 1981 against Swansea City. He also became the first black player to score for the club, doping so against Middlesbrough on 21st October 1981.

A69. Manchester United, then known as Newton Heath, played their first league match at Bank Street against Burnley on 1st September 1893, when 10,000 people saw Alf Farman score a hat-trick in a 3-2 win.

A70. Manchester United finished the 2018-19 season in a disappointing 6th position.

Here is the next batch of questions.

71. Who is the longest serving captain of
    Manchester United?
    A. Roy Keane
    B. Bryan Robson
    C. Nemanja Vidić

72. What nationality is Anthony Martial?
    A. Belgian
    B. French
    C. German

73. Who did Manchester United beat in the 2017
    Europa League Final?
    A. Anderlecht
    B. Ajax
    C. Juventus

74. What is the club's longest unbeaten run in a
    league campaign?
    A. 25 matches
    B. 27 matches
    C. 29 matches

75. Who won FIFA World Player of the Year
    whilst a Manchester United player?
    A. Eric Cantona
    B. Bryan Robson
    C. Cristiano Ronaldo

Here is the latest set of answers.

A71. The longest-serving captain is Bryan Robson, who was club captain from 1982 to 1994, although he held the position jointly with Steve Bruce from 1992 to 1994.

A72. Anthony Martial is French.

A73. Manchester United beat Ajax Amsterdam 2-0 in the 2017 Europa League Final held in Stockholm on 24th May 2017.

A74. Manchester United's longest unbeaten run in the League is 29 matches. This lasted from 26th December 1998 to 25th September 1999 and also from 11th April 2010 to 5th February 2011.

A75. Cristiano Ronaldo won the FIFA World Player of the Year award while playing for Manchester United in 2008.

76. Which of these songs is unique to Manchester United?
    A. Tuppence a bag
    B. Twenty Times
    C. Two Little Boys

77. When was the Munich Air Disaster?
    A. 1954
    B. 1956
    C. 1958

78. In 2000, Old Trafford was chosen as the venue for the final for which competition?
    A. Junior Athletics
    B. Rugby League World Cup
    C. Twenty20 Cricket

79. Which of these players are on the statue of the club's "Holy Trinity"?
    A. George Best, Denis Law and Bobby Charlton
    B. Joe Cassidy, Denis Law and Bob Donaldson
    C. Charlie Moore, Denis Law and Eric Cantona

80. Who holds the record for the shortest debut in the club's history?
    A. Frank Barrett
    B. Nicholas Culkin
    C. Jack Peddie

A76. Manchester United fans have a song which cannot be sung by anyone else. It is "Twenty times, twenty times, Man United, playing football the Matt Busby way."

A77. The Munich air disaster occurred on February 6th 1958 at 3 minutes past 3 in the afternoon when British European Airways flight 609 crashed on its third attempt to take off from a slush covered runway. Of the 44 people on the plane, there were 23 fatalities.

A78. Old Trafford was chosen as the venue for the 2000 Rugby League World Cup Final, and the match was contested by Australia and New Zealand.

A79. On 29th May 2008, to celebrate the 40th anniversary of Manchester United's first European Cup title, a statue of the club's "Holy Trinity" of George Best, Denis Law and Bobby Charlton, was unveiled across Sir Matt Busby Way from the East Stand, directly opposite the statue of Busby.

A80. We are reliably informed that the shortest debut in the club's history is Nicholas Culkin whose first United match was on their Scandinavian tour, before the 1997–98 season. He came on for the last few minutes for Manchester United's first choice goalkeeper, Peter Schmeichel.

Here is the next set of questions.

81. In 1997, why did Manchester United have to play a home European game in Plymouth?
    A. Bad weather
    B. European ban
    C. Old Trafford was being renovated

82. What was the name given to the group who progressed from the club's youth team into the first team in the 1950s?
    A. The Busby Babes
    B. The Busby Boys
    C. The Busby Brutes

83. What was George Best's nickname?
    A. El Beatle
    B. The Rising Star
    C. Super George

84. What award was given to Peter Schmeichel in 1992 and 1993?
    A. World's best goalkeeper
    B. World's biggest hands
    C. World's strangest haircut

85. Who was the first Manchester United player to win the European Footballer of the Year?
    A. Bobby Charlton
    B. Denis Law
    C. Cristiano Ronaldo

Here is the next set of answers.

A81. UEFA made United play the Cup Winners' Cup First Round 2nd leg match on 5th October 1997 at Plymouth Argyle's ground as punishment for the "violence" at a European game in Saint Etienne in France. At the time French bakers were on strike and some United supporters teased the home supporters by throwing bread at them.

A82. Under the management of Sir Matt Busby, The Busby Babes were notable not only for being young and gifted, but for being developed by the club itself, rather than bought from other clubs, which was customary then, as now.

A83. Best was catapulted to superstar status at the age of 19 when he scored two goals in a European Cup quarter-final match against Benfica in Lisbon on 9 March 1966. The Portuguese media dubbed him "The fifth Beatle", and on the team's return to England, George was photographed in his new sombrero with the headline, "El Beatle".

A84. Peter Schmeichel was voted the "World's Best Goalkeeper" in 1992 and 1993.

A85. Denis Law was the first Manchester United player to win the Ballon d'Or (European Footballer of the Year) – winning it in 1964.

86. What is the most number of points the club
    has achieved in a Premier League season?
    A. 90
    B. 91
    C. 92

87. What shirt number does Victor Lindelof wear?
    A. 2
    B. 12
    C. 20

88. What is Manchester United's official website?
    A. Manutd.com
    B. MUFC.com
    C. Reddevils.com

89. Which Manchester united player was once
    booked for a foul committed by his brother?
    A. Fábio Da Silva
    B. Will Keane
    C. Phil Neville

90. Which player scored in extra time of the last
    ever FA Cup semi-final replay in 1999?
    A. Eric Cantona
    B. Mark Hughes
    C. Ryan Giggs

A86. The highest number of points achieved is 92 in 42 matches, in the 1993–94 Premier League season.

A87. Swedish defender Victor Lindelof wears shirt number 2.

A88. manutd.com is the official Manchester United website providing news, online ticket sales, live match commentary, video highlights, player profiles etc. etc.

A89. On 27th October 2009, Fábio Da Silva was booked for a foul committed by his twin brother Rafael in United's 2–0 League Cup victory over Barnsley. Manchester United appealed and The Football Association agreed it was a case of mistaken identity, transferring the card to Rafael.

A90. On 14th April 1999, in the last ever FA Cup semi-final replay, Ryan Giggs scored in the last minute of extra time to help the club defeat Arsenal 2-1 at Villa Park. The goal was later voted the greatest ever goal scored in FA Cup history.

91. Whose corner kicks helped United win the 1999 Champions League Final?
    A. David Beckham
    B. Nicky Butt
    C. Teddy Sheringham

92. Which shirt number was famously worn by George Best, Eric Cantona and Bryan Robson?
    A. 7
    B. 8
    C. 10

93. What was the score of the Manchester United v Arsenal league match of August 2011?
    A. 6-2
    B. 7-2
    C. 8-2

94. In 2003 which player was involved in a dressing room argument with Alex Ferguson resulting in an injury to the player's face?
    A. David Beckham
    B. Andrew Cole
    C. Dwight Yorke

95. Which of these spent his entire football career at Manchester United?
    A. Nicky Butt
    B. Phil Neville
    C. Paul Scholes

A91. In the Champions League final on 26th May 1999 at the Camp Nou Stadium in Barcelona, Manchester United were losing the match 1-0 at the end of normal time, but went on to win the trophy 2-1 by scoring two goals in injury time. Both of the goals came from corners taken by David Beckham. Who could ever forget it?

A92. The iconic number 7 shirt has been worn by many Manchester United greats such as George Best, Johnny Berry, Steve Coppell, Bryan Robson, Eric Cantona, David Beckham, Cristiano Ronaldo, Antonio Valencia and even Angel de Maria.

A93. In August 2011, Arsenal suffered their heaviest league defeat in 84 years as they lost 8–2 to Manchester United at Old Trafford. Arsenal had not lost a league game by such a margin since 1927.

A94. In 2003, Ferguson was involved in a dressing room argument with David Beckham, resulting in an injury to Beckham, which was alleged to have been caused by Ferguson kicking a football boot in frustration which hit the player in the face.

A95. Paul Scholes spent his entire career at Manchester United.

Here is the final set of questions. Enjoy!

96. Who moved to Liverpool in 1964?
     A. Phil Chisnall
     B. Pat Crerand
     C. Paul Ince

97. Which United player received the most red cards in his career at Manchester United?
     A. Darren Fletcher
     B. Roy Keane
     C. John O'Shea

98. Which is considered the most successful season in Manchester United's history?
     A. 1996-97
     B. 1997-98
     C. 1998-99

99. Who was the captain of Manchester United when they acclaimed a treble of trophies?
     A. Steve Bruce
     B. Rio Ferdinand
     C. Roy Keane

100.   Alex Ferguson was the very first winner of the Premier League Manager of the Month award in which season?
     A. 1992-93
     B. 1993–94
     C. 1994–95

101.   In which city did Manchester United beat Chelsea to win the Champions League trophy in 2008?
    A. Madrid
    B. Munich
    C. Moscow

Here is the final set of answers.

A96. Since the 1964 transfer of Phil Chisnall from United to Liverpool; no player has been transferred directly between the two clubs. Some players, however, have played for both clubs, but having played elsewhere between, such as Paul Ince.

A97. Roy Keane received his first red card as a Manchester United player in a 2-0 FA Cup semi-final replay win against Crystal Palace, after stamping on Gareth Southgate. This incident was the first of a staggering eleven red cards Keane would accumulate in his United career.

A98. The 1998–99 season was the most successful season in the history of Manchester United Football Club. United won a treble of trophies (the Premier League, FA Cup and Champions League), thus becoming the first and only side in English football history to achieve such a feat.

A99. During the 1998–99 season, Roy Keane was captain of the United team that won The Treble - the Premier League, FA Cup and Champions League, a unique feat in English football.

A100. Ferguson was the very first winner of the Premier League Manager of the Month award, introduced for the start of the 1993–94 season, when he collected the accolade for August 1993.

A101. Manchester United won the 2008 Champions League Trophy in Moscow; when Chelsea captain John Terry unluckily slipped whilst taking his spot kick that could have won the trophy for the Blues.

That's it. I hope you enjoyed this book, and I hope you got most of the answers right.

I also hope you learnt some new facts about the club, and if you saw anything wrong, or have a general comment, please visit the glowwormpress.com website.

Thanks for reading, and if you did enjoy the book, would you please leave a positive review on Amazon.

CPSIA information can be obtained
at www.ICGtesting.com
Printed in the USA
LVHW010755180120
643990LV00003B/62